a *flowmotion*™ title

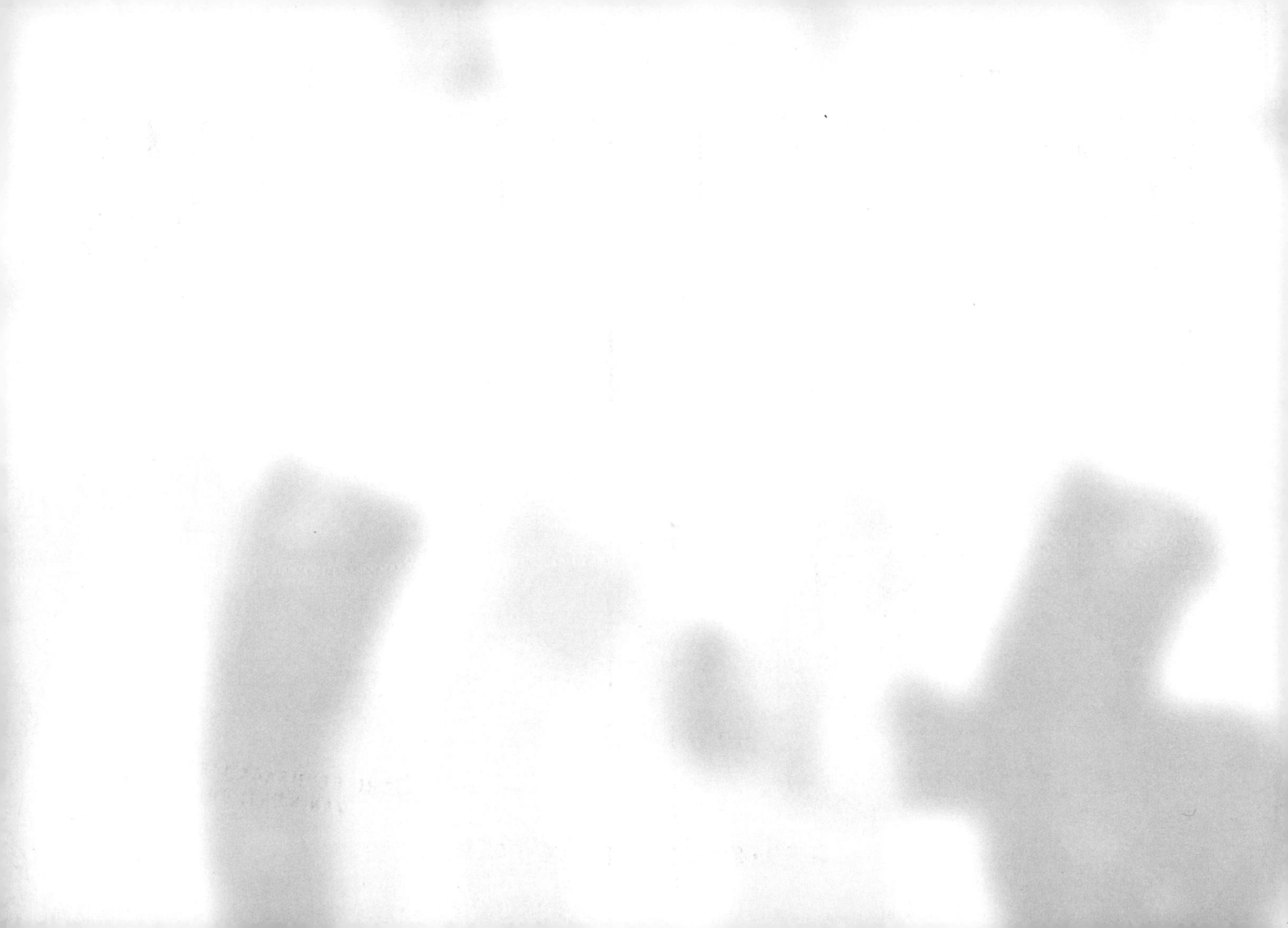

swing dancing

simon selmon

Sterling Publishing Co., Inc.
New York

Created and conceived by
Axis Publishing Limited
8c Accommodation Road
London NW11 8ED
www.axispublishing.co.uk

Creative Director: Siân Keogh
Managing Editor: Brian Burns
Project Designer: Anna Knight
Project Editor: Madeleine Jennings
Production Manager: Sue Bayliss
Photographer: Mike Good

Library of Congress Cataloging-in-Publication
Data Available

10 9 8 7 6 5 4 3 2 1

Published in 2002 by Sterling Publishing Co., Inc.
387 Park Avenue South, New York, NY 10016

Distributed in Canada by Sterling Publishing
c/o Canadian Manda Group,
One Atlantic Avenue, Suite 105
Toronto, Ontario, M6K 3E7, Canada

Separation by
United Graphics Pte Limited
Printed and bound by
Star Standard (Pte) Limited

Sterling ISBN 0–8069–9300–4

a *flowmotion*™ title

swing dancing

contents

introduction

why swing?

Flowmotion Swing introduces you to a whole new world of modern social dancing, as danced today in swing clubs from New York and Los Angeles to Paris, Stockholm, and London. Packed full of useful tips and facts, this book is an essential resource for teachers and dancers alike. Readers can move at their own pace and review sections as often as they like.

Any new skill takes time and discipline but, with a willingness to learn Swing dancing, progress can be fast. Before you know it, we will have you swingin' out, swayin, peckin', doing the Texas Tommy, and spinning at parties, clubs, and any function where there's a Swing band or DJ. And as well as being lots of fun, it's also good exercise.

the history of swing

Like Jazz music, Swing dance is a gumbo of people's experiences. African and West Indian musical heritage and formal European traditions melted together to give Swing music and dance its colorful history.

Our story of Swing begins with Ragtime: a cheerful music that soon gained popularity all over America. It also journeyed across the Atlantic to London, Paris, and the rest of Europe. Its popularity lasted from the end of the 19th century for almost two decades (until 1917). With Ragtime came the Cakewalk: a dance with strong African-American roots, which had an energetic and exaggerated strutting style and was soon the rage everywhere. It was followed by the animal dances, such as the Turkey Trot, Grizzly Bear, and Bunny Hug. These, along with scores of other energetic dances, soon found their way into the fashionable ballrooms of

This move is the end of the Lindy Turn, showing the swing out.

the day. They broke away from previous traditional European dances of the ballroom, like the Waltz. They allowed for much closer contact than previously seen on a dance floor, and were condemned by the church and polite society. But to quote a famous song of the day, "Everybody's Doing It."

from ragtime to jazz

As vaudeville acts and shows traveled around the United States, the popular "dance act" would spread these new dances; and on their travels would pick up new steps and ideas that would constantly develop the dance, for as audiences quickly tired of the old dances, new ones had to be devised.

"The Jazz Age" came about in the 1920s. Fueled by Prohibition (1920-1933), when alcohol was more or less banned in the U.S., "speakeasies" run by mobsters and bootleggers served plenty of alcohol and "hot jazz." Within this unique set of circumstances, new dances were born, such as the Charleston and Black Bottom. The Charleston was a hit number in the 1923 show *Running Wild* and the Black Bottom was introduced to the general public in the show *Scandals of 1926*. Like the Cakewalk, both of these dance crazes started life as wild, energetic affairs that had to be tamed for the ballroom. They were both important influences on the early Lindy Hop.

During the Ragtime era and the Jazz Age, other dances were also developing, such as the Texas Tommy and the Breakaway, both of which contributed to the Lindy. The Texas Tommy was a close-contact couple dance in which, after a few basic steps, the lady is literally whirled out and back in again. The Breakaway allowed partners to separate and do their own thing before coming back together. Along with the Hop, these dances were all forerunners of the Lindy.

Around 1924, a new sound emerged—Swing. Banjos were replaced with guitars, tubas with the bass, and clarinets with saxophones. A compelling 4/4 timing emerged from the rhythm section. New York, particularly Harlem, replaced Chicago as the jazz center. As the Jazz Age finally drew to a close about the time of the Great Depression of 1929, the Swing era was waiting in the wings to replace it. It was at this point that the Lindy Hop emerged—a dance that mixed Charleston steps with breakaways and all kinds of jazz steps. Its influence was far reaching.

cool styles in swing

EAST COAST SWING: The latest of the three dances, great for 50s Rock 'n' Roll and Rhythm & Blues, is East Coast Swing. This is a 6-count dance. The emergence of Rhythm & Blues in the late 40s and early 50s brought a new way to Lindy. Lindy changed from being mostly 8 count or 8 and 6 count to being primarily just 6 count. Simplified to match the music, which now had a heavier emphasis on the beat and fewer musicians, Swing dancing was now anything performed to Swing, Rock 'n' Roll, and Rhythm & Blues.

Although the name Lindy was still being used in the United States during the 50s in dance schools, which had become popular places to learn and dance, they wanted to call their simplified swing East Coast Swing to differentiate it from the more complicated 8-count Lindy steps. Meanwhile, in England a similar environment produced Ballroom Jive.

We have chosen to teach you East Coast Swing first because it is so quick and easy to pick up, is great for dancing to 50s style Rock 'n' Roll music, and it is an ideal way to start learning the Lindy.

LINDY HOP: Often called America's national dance, Lindy Hop is the original jazzy, partnered dance consisting of 8- and 6-count patterns. Lindy is made up of hundreds of individual steps, breaks, and variations. Like call and response in Jazz music (in which one musician plays a line and another or others respond), so do Lindy Hoppers respond to the music as well as each other. It is a dance that constantly grows and adapts to its environment (this can be seen by the addition of some street and hip hop movements from some of today's younger practitioners).

The dance was made popular in Britain during World War II by American GIs, and subsequently adopted the name "Jitterbug." It was (and still is) danced to the original big band music of the 30s and 40s, but today bands such as Big Bad Voodoo Daddy and the Royal Crown Review offer a modern-day brand of "neo-swing" music to dance to.

HOLLYWOOD SWING: During the 30s and 40s, a swing dance style was developing in the West Coast, particularly Los Angeles. Los Angeles attracted residents from all over seeking their fortunes in Hollywood's booming film industry. They brought with them among other things their musical and dancing influences. Two dances that heavily influenced this future Swing dance were the 30s Balboa and Shag. The most influential and famous dancer of that period was Dean Collins, who can be seen dancing in numerous movies from the 40s, often with dance partner Jewel McGowan. Dean moved from New York to Los Angeles in the late 1930s and brought with him dances from the Savoy Ballroom. His smooth style Lindy Hop influenced many dancers during that period and is becoming popular once again among today's new generation of Swing dancers.

TIMING TERMINOLOGY

Musically, Swing is made up of beats and bars. There are four beats to a bar. A dancer will count slow (S) as two beats of music, and Quicks (Q) as one beat of music.

The slows can be further subdivided into single steps (one step or weight change), or triple steps (three steps or two weight changes), or kick step (kick down), all of which happen in two beats of music. When we describe a single step taking two beats of music (i.e. slow), this can often be interchanged with a triple step or a kick step.

For example, a Lindy Turn takes eight beats (or two bars of music) and can be danced with QQSQQS = 1+1+2+1+1+2 = 8 beats.
A typical six-count basic consists of QQSS = 1+1+2+2 =6 beats or a Rock Step followed by two triples.

When dancing many Lindy Hop and Hollywood Swing moves, such as the Lindy Turn and Whip Leader and Follower, triple timing is frequently used.

MAN'S EXAMPLE

Start with your back step (two steps left, right—QQ) on beat one, beat two. Substitute three steps (two weight changes) in place of one single step on your left foot (slow) i.e., stepping on your left foot for beat three and beat four becomes left, right, left with the timing three and four.
Step right on beat five (Q)
Step left on beat six (Q)
Replace a single step on your right foot (S) on beat seven and eight with right, left, right on beats seven and eight.

WOMAN'S EXAMPLE

Start with your back step (two steps right, left—QQ) on beat one and beat two.

Substituting three steps (two weight changes) in place of one single step on your right foot (S) i.e., stepping on your right foot for beat three, and beat four becomes right, left, right with the timing three and four.
Step left on beat five (Q)
Step right on beat six (Q)
Replace a single step on your left foot (S) on beat seven and beat eight with left, right, left on beat seven and eight.

This is a classic look for the Lindy Hop. Both are wearing 40s suits—his is double breasted and set off with two-tone shoes.

music and musicality

What makes one dancer stand out from others—usually it's their musicality. Some people just seem to have it; others may need to spend a little time learning this new language. To understand timing and to learn where the beat or backbone of a song comes from, you don't need to be a trained musician. Just listen to some music and try to pick out the rhythm section (Drums, Bass, Guitar, Piano). That's what musically drives the band along. Clap or tap your foot to the beat and try to isolate the separate instruments.

This is a classic Hollywood Swing look. The man is wearing baggy zoot suit pants, which are high-waisted and tapered at the bottom, and a wide 40s tie. The woman is wearing a casual skirt and top, sneakers and bobby sox, and a flower in the hair for a touch of glamour.

typical tunes you could hear at a good dance

With a choice of music from eight decades to dance to, enjoy it all.

NICE AND EASY FOR DANCING—these tunes are good to practice to because they give you lots of time to play and improvize:

Shiny Stockings—Count Basie and His Orchestra

Tuxedo Junction—Erskin Hawkins and His Orchestra

Blues for Stephanie—George Gee and His Make Believe Ballroom Orchestra

When My Sugar Walks Down the Street—Oscar Peterson

Shout Sister Shout—Sister Rosetta Tharpe

Oops, My Bad!—Yalloppin' Hounds

I Love Being Here With You—Diana Krall

GUARANTEED TO FILL A DANCE FLOOR

One O'Clock Jump—Count Basie and His Orchestra

Take the "A" Train—Duke Ellington and His Orchestra

In the Mood—Glenn Miller and His Orchestra (Listen to the original and accept no imitations.)

Tain't What You Do—Jimmie Lunceford

Gotta Pebble in My Shoe—Chick Webb with Ella Fitzgerald

Second Era of Swing—Pete Jacobs and His Wartime Radio Review
You've Got What it Takes—Steve Lucky and the Rumba Bums
Swingin' the Century—Bill Elliott Swing Orchestra
Yacht Club Swing—Fats Waller
Zoot Suit—Bob Crosby
Watch the Birdie—Lisa Stansfield
Stompin' at the Savoy—Benny Goodman

UP THE TEMPO, ROLL BACK THE CARPET, IT'S TIME TO LET OFF STEAM!

Rock Around the Clock—Bill Haley
Boogie Woogie Country Girl—Big Joe Turner
Beat Me Daddy 8 to the Bar—Andrew Sisters
Mildred Won't You Behave—Bill Elliot Swing Orchestra
Big Time Operator—Big Bad Voodoo Daddy
Sing, Sing, Sing—Benny Goodman
Jumping at the Woodside—Count Basie and His Orchestra
(Be warned: don't expect to last the whole song on these last two!)

CLASSIC HAND POSITIONS

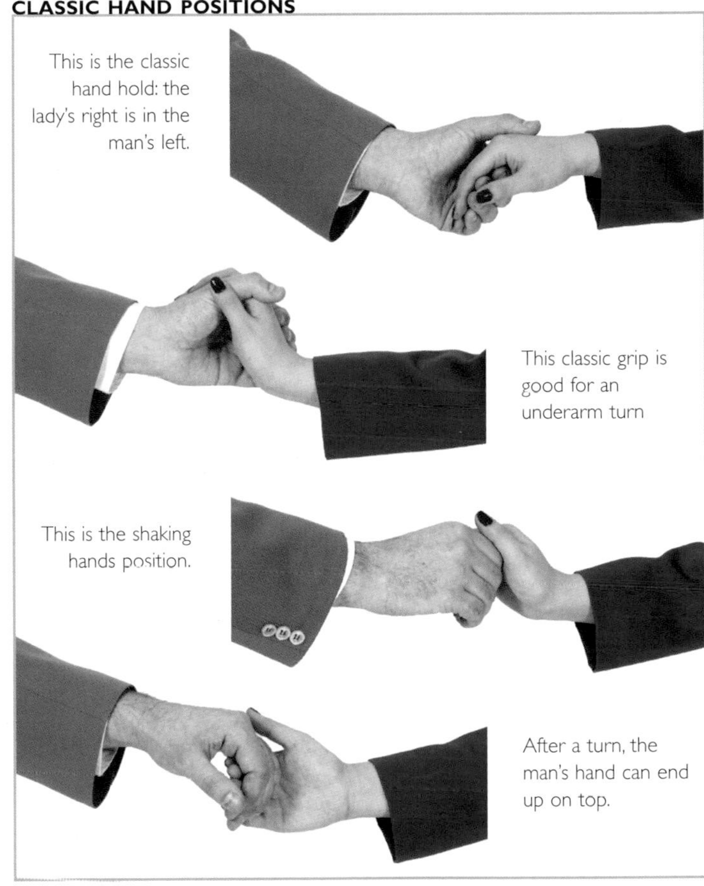

This is the classic hand hold: the lady's right is in the man's left.

This classic grip is good for an underarm turn

This is the shaking hands position.

After a turn, the man's hand can end up on top.

swing for everyone

What makes Lindy so accessible to so many people is that you can put as much or as little effort into the dance as you want. The young and energetic can throw each other around all night long, while others may prefer a nice and relaxed style with simple steps. What's so great is they can all share the dance floor at the same time. Lindy Hop can be as wild as your imagination or as relaxed and carefree as your mood. Primarily a social dance that anyone can do, it can be taken to performance level as seen in countless movies, shows, and competitions. Lindy is based around its rhythm and partnering skills, and therefore almost anything goes if it's in time with the music and has the basic patterns as its framework. Like jazz, there is lots of room for improvizing once the basics have been mastered.

consideration for others

Swing dancing is a social dance that is all about teamwork; you need good lead and follow skills, and the right amount of connection, resistance, and tension between two people. At times it's almost as if there is a mirror between you, and just a little subtle pressure will decide the outcome of a movement. So you need the ability to listen to your partner. All this requires trust on both sides and an awareness of those around you. You won't have a very long dancing career if you are inconsiderate to others dancing around you. If you bump into somebody (even if it's not your fault), a quick sorry and a smile are just common courtesy. Generally, it's polite to accept most invitations to dance, but don't feel obliged to accept. It's always OK to say "not right now, thank you." Generally, all the skills you need in everyday life apply on the dance floor.

different terms

Since the dance spans more than eight decades, there is often a confusion over some of the various terms used. Lindy Hop was the dance that was performed to Swing music, and the golden era of Swing was 1935–45. Lindy Hoppers, Jitterbugs, and Bobby Soxers were the dancers. In Harlemese speak, or Jive talk, another name for a Jitterbug was Alligator, and these Alligators—also known as Jitterbugs or Swing fans—were also Rug cutters, otherwise known as Active Jitterbugs. As the dance changed, we got East Coast Swing and Hollywood Swing, to name but a few. All these different styles are referred to today under the umbrella of Swing Dance.

DO'S AND DON'TS OF SWING

don't get caught up on steps: it's style that counts

have a sense of humor

the steps' offbeat character and their jazz background give them style; now you must give them attitude

have timing, timing, timing

don't forget to drink while dancing (But a vast quantity of alcohol is not what I am referring to!)

Airsteps (one partner leaves the ground) and when they are used:
Jam circles (when dancers form a circle to let one couple come out and "shine")—Yes!
Competitions—Yes! (but read the rules first!)
Performance—Yes!
Social setting—No!

Only use an airstep once you have practiced it enough in a safe environment. It's very tempting to want to show off, but it can lead to a very short and painful dancing career. Never try airsteps, dips, or drops when you are tired or with a partner who is not expecting them.

Standing in the neutral position.

"Getting down" or hitting the "frog" position in the Lindy Hop.

The "fencing" position for Hollywood Swing.

do's and don'ts of swing

The classic Back Step (or Rock Step) position. This shows good connection with the weight nicely balanced over their own feet.

Not so good! Their arms are too extended. Leaning back, pulling too far away from each other is dangerous on a crowded dance floor.

far left: A case of "where are you?" Notice that they are not facing each other.

left: And now they are—in the correct face-off position.

The correct close-hold position, with the woman's left arm on the man's right shoulder, his right arm under her shoulder blade—and not squeezing too tight.

Definitely not right—a classic case of "Mr. Wandering Hand" about to get into trouble.

go with the flow

The special Flowmotion images used in this book have been created to allow you to see the whole dance sequence, not just selected highlights. The images in each sequence run from left to right and illustrate how to get into each part of the dance in a detailed and accurate manner. The captions along the bottom of the images provide supplementary information to help you with the moves. Below this is the time line, another level of information, which gives you instructions for counting the steps and beats.

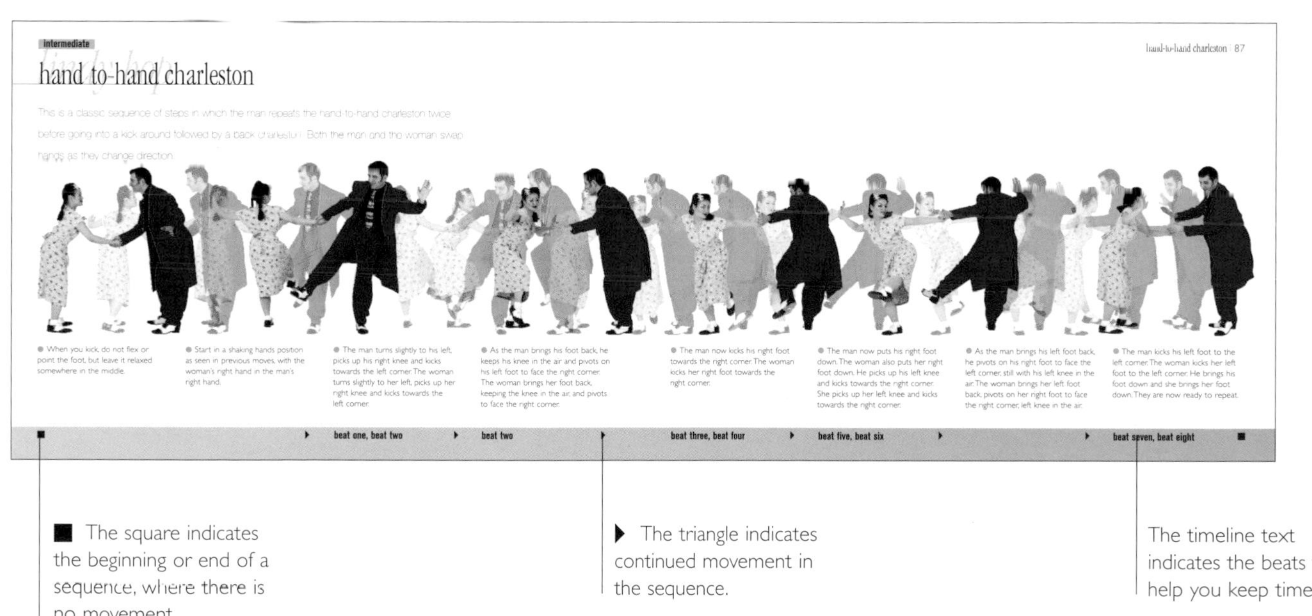

■ The square indicates the beginning or end of a sequence, where there is no movement.

▶ The triangle indicates continued movement in the sequence.

The timeline text indicates the beats to help you keep time.

east coast swing

six-count basic—man

east coast swing

The Lindy six-count basic goes one, two (slow), three, four (slow), five (quick), six (quick). Put on some music, listen to the rhythm, and try these steps continuously. Follow the music, keep the beat, and don't speed up halfway through. Keep both knees soft and lean forward with your weight over the balls of your feet. It may help to count out loud the first few times.

● Stand with both feet shoulder width apart. Relax, and let both arms float lightly away from your body, while keeping the elbows close, but not tight, to your waist.

● With your arms in the same position, shift your body weight onto your left foot for beat one and hold for beat two.

● At the same time, turn your body slightly in the direction of the foot you are stepping on.

● Then repeat on your right foot, stepping for beat three and holding for beat four.

● The next step—a Back Step—involves stepping back on beat five onto your left foot, and keeping the supporting knee bent, with your right knee slightly raised.

● Then step back onto your front foot (right), facing your partner on beat six.

● Once the weight has fully transferred onto your right foot, you have completed the move.

beat three, beat four ▶ **beat five** ▶ **beat six** ▶ **beat six**

six-count basic—woman

east coast swing

The basic timing is the same as for the man, but remember to follow his rhythm, not the music. If he loses the rhythm, then lose it with him. It's better for both of you to dance out of time together than for just one of you to be moving to the correct rhythm.

● As with your partner, start with both feet about shoulder width apart. Relax and let both arms float lightly away from your body, while keeping the elbows close, but not tight, to your waist.

● With your arms in the same position, shift your body weight onto your right foot for beat one and hold for beat two.

● At the same time, turn your body slightly in that direction of the foot you are stepping on.

● Then repeat on your left foot, stepping for beat three and holding for beat four.

● The next step—a Back Step—involves stepping back on beat five onto your right foot, while keeping the supporting knee bent, with your right knee slightly raised.

● Then step back onto your front foot (left) on beat six, as if facing your partner.

● When the weight has fully transferred onto your left foot, you have completed the move.

beat three, beat four ▶ **beat five** ▶ ▶ **beat six** ■

six-count basic—in open hold

east coast swing

Practice these steps again—remembering to look at your partner and not at the floor. And smile—if you do, your partner will, too. Now that you have a basic footwork pattern and rhythm, it is time to take hold of your partner. Practice these moves continuously, first without and then with music.

● The man leads by taking the woman's right hand firmly in his left—without gripping too tightly. They start quite close because they will have to Back Step away from each other.

● The man steps onto his left foot. The woman follows by stepping onto her right foot.

● The man stays close to the woman and keeps his hand at more or less waist level.

● The man steps onto his right foot. The woman follows by stepping onto her left foot.

● The man steps back onto his left foot and pushes his left arm forward, firmly, smoothly and evenly, without jerking it. This is the woman's lead to step straight back onto her right foot.

● The woman matches the man's arm movements. If he bends his, she bends hers. If he extends his, she extends hers.

● The man then pulls the woman back toward him, while shifting his weight once more onto his right foot (front). The woman follows by shifting her weight onto her left foot (front).

beat three, beat four ▶ **beat five** ▶ **beat five** ▶ **beat six** ▶

transition to close hold

The close hold position is similar to the classic ballroom position. However, it has a more relaxed frame—the elbows are down as opposed to out rigidly to the side (as they would be in ballroom dancing).

● Having completed beats five and six of the six count basic in open position, you are ready to continue.

● While the man steps forward onto his left foot, he leads the woman forward onto her right foot. They are now leaning in toward each other.

● The woman rests her left arm on his right shoulder. The man slips his right hand—keeping it flat—around her back, placing it just under her left shoulder blade. His left arm is at waist level, nice and relaxed.

take hold ▶ **beat one, beat two** ▶

The man then shifts his weight onto his right foot, and the woman follows by shifting onto her left foot. He then gently pulls her toward him so that his right side is close to her left side.

The woman rests her left arm on on the man's shoulder, where she can feel his body move backward and forward.

beat three, beat four

The man then takes a Back Step at a slight angle, with his left foot behind his right. The woman takes a Back Step, with her right foot slightly behind her left.

beat five

When making a Back Step, the man is careful to keep the arm around the woman's back close to him. As he leads with his left hand, he steps back with his left foot.

beat six

east coast swing

tuck turn

This step, also known as Turn the Lady Under. A tip worth remembering for the man is to let the woman's fingers rotate loosely inside your hand. Don't stir her arm around.

● Start with the man's right arm around the woman's back, her left arm on his right shoulder, and her right foot between his feet.

● To start, complete one basic in close hold and finish in close hold position with a Back Step.

● The man steps forward onto his left foot while raising his left hand above the woman's head.

● The woman steps forward onto her right foot, with her right hand pushing into the man's left.

● When the man lifts his arm—and the woman's—this gives the signal for a turn. He guides the woman under his left arm with his right hand on the woman's back; his left hand acts as a central axis above her head.

● The woman pivots all the way around on her right foot, closing her left foot to right. The man closes his right foot to the left.

beat three, beat four ▶ ▶

● The man then steps back onto his left foot while lowering his left arm and pushing it toward the woman's waist. She steps back onto her right foot, raising her right knee a little and keeping the left knee slightly bent.

beat five ▶

● The man then puts his weight back onto his right foot while pulling the woman toward him. She follows by putting her weight back onto her left foot.

beat six ▶

changing places

This move will go a lot more smoothly if, when changing places, you don't grip each other's hands, but instead let the man's fingers rotate loosely inside the woman's hand.

● This move follows on immediately from beats five and six of the previous turn under.

● The man's weight is back onto his right foot, her weight is back onto her left foot.

● The man steps forward on his left foot, while using his left hand to pull the woman past his right hip.

● The woman steps straight forward on her right foot as she feels herself being led past the man.

● The man raises his left arm above the woman's head, and she begins to turn.

● The man then turns approximately 180 degrees to the right, closing his right foot to the left.

● The woman waits until the man lowers his right hand over her head and turns her 180 degrees to the left to face him.

● The man lowers his left hand and leads the Back Step. The woman waits for his lead.

▶ **beat three, beat four** ▶ **beat three, beat four** ▶ **beat five, beat six** ▶

american spin

The American spin, sometimes known as a push spin, is a very common move in swing dance. A tip for the woman is to "spot," or look at your partner both before and after he spins you.

● Start in an open-hold basic. Complete one six-count basic, finishing with a Back Step.

● The man steps slightly forward (almost on the spot) onto his right foot. The woman steps forward onto her left foot.

● The man pulls the woman toward him, checking her forward movement with his left hand in preparation for a turn.

● The woman should have a feeling of heaviness in her right arm as she pushes into the man's hand.

● The man closes his right foot to the left and pushes down with his left hand toward the woman's center, enabling her to turn. He lets go with his left hand.

● At this forward signal, the woman spins with her weight centered over the ball of her right foot and turns to her right. She then closes left to right as she finishes the turn before placing her weight back onto her left foot.

● The man catches the woman's right hand in his left and leads the Back Step.

beat three, beat four ▶ ▶ **beat three, beat four** ▶ **beat five, beat six** ■

free changing places

This move is also known as a "right side pass." When the man releases the woman's right hand, she must remember to leave it out so he can get hold of it again to continue.

● Start with a Back Step (beat one, beat two) in an open hold, with the woman's right hand in the man's left.

● As the man replaces the weight onto his right foot, he pulls the woman forward to his right side.

● He steps forward onto his left foot with his left arm across his body, being careful not to knock the woman with his right elbow.

● The woman steps forward onto her right foot as he passes her, keeping her right arm close to her waist and bent at the elbow.

● The man lets go of the woman's right hand as they both continue to turn. After the turn, he catches her right hand again with his left hand, having stepped onto his right foot.

● As the woman steps forward onto her left foot, her right hand trails around the man's back until he catches hold of it again.

● The man and woman face each other to end with a Back Step in an open-hold position.

beat five, beat six

she goes he goes

To help this move go more smoothly, any time you are changing places under your partner, you should allow your fingers to rotate loosely inside your partner's hand.

● Start with a Back Step on beat one, beat two in an open hold, with the woman's right hand in the man's left.

● As the man steps forward on the left foot, he raises his left arm, bending it at the elbow and pulling the woman toward his right side.

● The woman steps forward onto her right foot, going past the man.

beat one, beat two ▶

beat three, beat four ▶

beat three, beat four ▶

● As the man turns under his raised arm, he pivots on his left foot, turning over his left shoulder and finishing on his right foot facing his partner.

● The woman steps onto her left foot and turns a quarter turn to face her partner.

● The man then swaps hands in preparation for the next move.

● As the man prepares to take his next Back Step, he has picked up the woman's right hand with his right hand and they finish in a shaking hands position.

beat five ▶ **beat five** ▶ **beat six** ▶ **beat six** ■

east coast swing

change places behind back

This is a genuine piece of '50s cool. When the man gets really good at this—with a bit of practice—he shouldn't even have to look at his partner.

● Begin with the woman's right hand in the man's right—the shaking hands position.

● The man and woman start changing places by taking a Back Step away from each other.

● The man steps forward onto his left foot, pulling the woman past his right hip. She steps forward onto her right foot.

beat one

beat two

● The man keeps his body turning counterclockwise toward the woman. She finds herself turning slightly counterclockwise. He closes his right foot to left while continuing to face the woman as she goes past.

beat three, beat four ▶

● The woman continues turning counterclockwise, closing her left foot to right until she faces him again.

▶

● The man looks over his left shoulder to make sure he is not too close, changes hands behind his back, and turns to continue.

beat five, beat six ▶

● The man and woman now face each other once more to finish with a Back Step.

beat five, beat six ■

catapult

The number of beats in the catapult is equivalent to two six-count basics. A tip for the man is to let the woman "have the line" when she comes through—in other words, he gets out of her way so she can travel in a straight line.

● Start in a shaking hands position, with the woman's right hand in the man's right hand.

● Start with a Back Step on beat one, beat two.

● The man steps forward onto his left foot, pulling the woman past the right side of his body, with his hand pointing down.

● The man closes right to left, and the woman closes left to right. He catches her hands—right hand in right hand, left hand in left.

● The man steps fully forward onto his left foot and then replaces his weight back onto his right foot, pushing the woman back and then forward to create a catapult effect. He holds both her hands in his.

beat one, beat two ▶

● As the man pulls, the woman shoots past his left-hand side, stepping forward on her right foot. As she does so, he steps back onto his left foot, still pulling forward with a very slight downward motion.

beat three, beat four ▶

● When the woman passes the man, he turns her with the left hand so she completes a 360-degree turn.

beat five, beat six ▶

● The man steps on his right foot, the woman comes around to face him again, finishing her turn on her left foot, and the man takes her right hand in his left.

beat five, beat six ■

traveling kicks

Traveling kicks can be repeated any number of times. It can be done in a very small way, almost on the spot on a crowded dance floor, or high and covering a lot of floor where space permits.

● Start in a close-hold position, with the woman's right hand in the man's left, and his right arm around her waist.

● Begin with a Back Step on beat one, beat two to create some momentum.

● The man then pulls the woman closer toward him and kicks outside with his left foot. She kicks in between his legs with her right foot.

● Both lean over their kicking foot. As they put the kicking foot down, they turn away from each other.

beat one, beat two ▸ beat three, beat four ▸ ▸

● The man now turns to the left and kicks out with his right foot. The woman turns to the right and kicks out with her left foot.

● They then turn in toward each other and repeat the first kicks, the man kicking forward with his left foot and down. The woman kicks forward, and slightly inside, with her right and down.

● To begin the exit, like an underarm turn, the man now raises his left arm in preparation for turning the woman under, turning on the next kick down.

● The woman completes the turn over her right shoulder to face her partner again. The man finishes on his right foot, the woman on her left.

beat five, beat six ▶ **beat seven, beat eight** ▶ **beat one, beat two** ▶ **beat one, beat two** ■

the sway

Though the moves described here refer to catching the woman's arm, it doesn't really matter whether the man catches her by the hand or any other part of her arm.

● Start with a Back Step in a shaking-hands position, with the woman's right hand in the man's right.

● The man pulls the woman toward his right-hand side as he steps forward onto his left foot and catches hold of her left arm with his left hand. She steps forward, pivoting on her left foot, and around onto her right.

● The man then closes right to left and finishes with his right hand resting on the woman's right hip, both of them now facing the same direction. She closes left to right.

beat one, beat two ▶ **beat three, beat four** ▶ **beat five, beat six** ▶

● The man then sways the woman back to his right while stepping onto his left foot. She steps back onto her right foot, with her right shoulder swaying backward. He replaces his weight onto his right foot.

beat one, beat two ▶

● The man continues stepping forward onto his left foot and brings the woman's hip back in toward the center. She then replaces the weight forward onto her left foot, stepping forward on her right foot.

beat three, beat four

● As the man steps onto his right foot, he pushes the woman away with his left hand. As he does so, she turns approximately 180 degrees clockwise on her left foot to face the man.

beat five, beat six ▶

● Once she is fully facing him again, they finish with a Back Step as seen in previous moves.

beat six ■

hip lift

It's a very good idea here for the woman to bear in mind that when she jumps, she should jump right onto her partner. If she only jumps into his arms, he might not be able to support her.

Start in a close-hold position, side by side, with the man's right arm around the woman's waist.

Still in a close-hold position, they then take a Back Step as seen in previous moves.

The man steps onto his left foot and drops down slightly, preparing to lift the woman. He can use his left hand to take some of her weight.

beat one, beat two

beat three, beat four

● The woman goes down with him in prepartion to jump onto his hip. She can use both her arms to push down into the man for extra support.

● They both jump together, and he lifts her hip onto his right hip. As she jumps, she tucks her legs underneath to get her shins resting on the man's hip. At this point, they can hold a pose or exit immediately.

● To exit, the man bends his knees to get the momentum to lift the woman off his hip and supports her on the way down. When she is ready to exit, she will feel him bend his knees and throw her off.

● The woman should always land with her weight primarily over the ball of her foot and take a little bounce in the knees. They end in a side by-side position.

beat three, beat four ▶ **beat five, beat six** ▶ **beat seven, beat eight** ▶ ■

the monkey swing

For the woman, it helps if she keeps her chin tucked into her chest, pulls her shoulder back away from the floor, and doesn't sag in the middle, so that her hips do not hit the floor as she slides through the man's legs.

● Start with a shaking-hands grip but, this time, connected at the wrist. The woman uses her right hand, the man his left.

● The man pushes the woman away, and she then swings down between his legs.

● The man bends his knees and leans backward for counterbalance. The woman continues to slide between his legs, with her knees bent.

● The man then reaches down behind him with his left hand to catch the woman's right hand.

● The woman slides right through and begins to push up from her hips. Pushing up from her hips will make it a lot easier for her to stand up.

● The man helps to pull the woman upright. She looks up at him over her left shoulder as they both start to turn to face each other.

● They complete the turn and face each other, still connected at the wrist. They end with a Back Step.

▶ **beat five, beat six** ▶ **beat seven** ▶ **beat eight** ■

straddle

When the man comes to bending his knees, it helps to think of it as taking a small squat—keeping his back straight and using his legs. He should keep in mind timing, technique, and teamwork, particularly with regard to the jump.

● Start in an an open-hold position, with the woman's right hand in the man's left, and Back Step.

● The man steps in with his left foot, with feet parallel and at least shoulder width apart. The woman steps in on her right foot, bringing both feet together.

● The man bends his knees and places his hands around the woman's waist. She drops and places her forearms on his chest and shoulders, with her hands around the back of his neck, clasped or flat.

● They lift together. The woman jumps, and the man lifts her into a straddle position around his upper waist, her legs high up on each side of his chest. She squeezes her legs together, pulling her back and head up.

beat five, beat six ▶

● The man bends his knees while leaning forward slightly from the waist. The woman points her legs up.

beat seven, beat eight ▶

● The man pushes the woman up, lifting her at the waist as though he's trying to throw her away so that she can land. The woman helps by swinging backward, tucking in her legs and pushing her hips back and high.

beat one ▶

● The man can help support the woman as she lands. As before, the woman should land on the ball of the foot with a bounce in the knees.

beat two ■

lindy hop

lindy bop

lindy turn—man

The lindy turn is one of the classic moves that takes eight beats of music and is the basis of many of the variations that you will find in the pages that follow. Beats three and four, and beats seven and eight are frequently danced using the triple timing described on page 13.

● Start with a Back Step. As you step back, extend your left arm forward, bringing it back toward you as you replace your weight on your right foot.

● Step forward onto your left foot, continuing to pull your left arm in toward you. Begin to turn your body slightly clockwise. Keep the elbow tucked in and your hand at lower chest level.

● Bring your right forearm forward as if to place it under your partner's left shoulder blade. Imagine that you are parallel with, and facing, your partner.

beat one, beat two ▶ **beat three, beat four** ▶ ▶

● Keep your body nicely balanced over the foot you are stepping on. Don't step out too wide, and keep your knees soft at all times. Step behind with your right foot, turning slightly clockwise.

● Imagine, at the same time, that your right arm is pulling your partner around. As you step behind, finish by pulling your partner forward and past you.

● As the woman is passing you, release your right hand and continue to follow her around with your body, stepping around onto your left foot.

● Complete the turn as you close with your right foot to the left and down, once again facing your partner.

beat five ▶ ▶ **beat six** ▶ **beat seven, beat eight** ■

lindy turn—woman

The woman will find that each partner she dances with will probably lead this move slightly differently. But that's part of the fun—adapting to follow his lead. Most importantly for the woman, she must keep the eight-count rhythm while the man creates the position. Beats three and four, and seven and eight are frequently danced using the triple timing described on page 13.

● Starting with a Back Step, imagine that you are in an open hold with your partner.

● As the man extends his left arm forward, step back onto your right foot. As he begins to pull you toward him, replace the weight back on your left foot.

● As the man continues to pull you forward with his right arm, start stepping onto your right foot. As you do so, the man will begin to turn his body.

● You want to stay parallel and turn toward him, finishing with your left arm on his shoulder. To check you're in the correct position, your right toe should be pointing between the man's feet.

beat three, beat four ▶

● Now, continue stepping forward and around on your left foot.

beat five ▶

● Continue in a forward direction on your right foot, going past your partner.

beat six ▶

● Now, close left to right to turn back once again to face your partner.

beat seven, beat eight ■

lindy turn together

This is the most important move you can learn, and once you've mastered it, a number of variations are going to come much more easily. The lindy turn can be done at slower tempos, giving you time to improvise your footwork on the eight-count structure, or fast and furious for spectacular effect.

● Start with a Back Step. As the man steps back on his left foot, he extends his left arm forward, bringing it back toward him as he replaces his weight onto his right foot.

● As he does so, the woman steps back onto her right foot. As he begins to pull her forward, she replaces the weight onto her left foot.

● Stepping forward onto his left foot, the man pulls the woman in toward him and begins to turn clockwise. At the same time, he places his right hand under her left shoulder blade.

● As the man continues to pull the woman forward, she steps forward onto her right foot, turning her body parallel to his and placing her left hand on his right shoulder.

■ beat one, beat two | beat one, beat two ▸ | beat three, beat four ▸ | beat three, beat four ▸

● The man steps behind on his right foot and, with his right arm under the woman's left shoulder blade, he pulls her forward.

● When the woman feels his hand pulling on her back, she takes the first of two steps forward—on her left foot—in the direction of his pull.

● As the woman continues to step forward—now on her right foot—the man moves his right arm out of the way and steps around onto his left foot to face her.

● The man closes right to left to finish the turn and face his partner. The woman also turns to face the man, closing left to right.

beat five ▶ **beat five** ▶ **beat six** ▶ **beat seven, beat eight** ■

lindy turn styling

In this move, when the woman is doing the swivel right and swivel left, she must make sure that she is not stepping back as in the Back Step. When swiveling, she keeps her right hand pointing toward her partner. The bigger the swivels, the better it looks.

● Having completed one basic lindy turn, you can now begin your next turn, adding your lindy turn styling.

● On the Back Step, he leans forward with the top of his body while counterbalancing and kicking his left foot behind him for a long, lean look.

● On the Back Step, instead of the normal back replace, the woman swivels to the right and then swivels to the left.

● Stepping forward onto his left foot, the man pulls the woman in toward him and begins to turn clockwise. At the same time, he places his right hand under her left shoulder blade.

beat one, beat two ▶ **beat one, beat two** ▶ **beat three, beat four** ▶

● As the man continues to pull the woman forward, she steps forward onto her right foot, turning her body parallel to his and placing her left hand on his right shoulder.

● The man steps behind on his right foot, and with his right arm under the woman's left shoulder blade, he pulls her forward. When she feels his hand pulling on her, she takes the first of two steps forward—on her left foot.

● As the woman continues to step forward—now on her right foot—the man moves his right arm out of the way and steps around onto his left foot to face her.

● The man closes right to left to finish the turn and face his partner. The woman also turns to face the man, closing left to right.

beat three, beat four ▶ **beat five** **beat six** ▶ **beat seven, beat eight** ■

lindy circle

The lindy circle is a lindy turn in which you start in an open-hold position and finish in a closed position. The idea is for partners to stay fairly close to each other as they circle.

● Start with a Back Step in an open-hold position, with the woman's right hand in the man's left.

● As the man Back Steps on his left foot, he replaces his weight onto his right foot and begins to lead the woman forward.

● As the man steps forward onto his left foot, he places his right arm on her back under her right shoulder blade and pulls her in close.

● The woman steps forward onto her right foot. She moves in closer to put her left hand on the man's right shoulder.

■ beat one ▶ beat two ▶ beat three ▶

● The man steps behind with his right foot as they start to circle around. He continues the circle by stepping onto his left foot.

● The woman steps around onto her left foot; then her right foot. They stay in close hold as they complete a full circle.

● The man steps in place onto his right foot. The woman finishes the circle while stepping onto her left foot.

● They finish in a close hold, his right hand under her right shoulder blade and her right hand in his left hand, ready for another Back Step.

beat four ▶ **beat five** ▶ **beat six** ▶ **beat seven, beat eight** ■

charleston in open

In this move, the kicks don't have to be very high, and the idea is that the man and woman aim to be a mirror image of each other.

● Start in a close hold with the man's right arm around the woman's waist, in a side-by-side position. The woman has her weight on her left (inside) foot, and the man has his weight on his right (inside) foot.

● Leaning forward in an exaggerated fashion as they start the Back Step together, the man and the woman should swing their free arm forward.

● The man kicks his outside foot (left) forward and down. The woman kicks her outside foot (right) forward and down.

● As each of them brings their foot down, they pick up the other in preparation for the next step.

beat one, beat two ▶ beat three, beat four ▶

● The man and woman now double kick with their inside foot—his right, her left.

● The first kick for each is forward on beats five and six. As they do so, they continue swinging their outside arm for balance.

● The second kick for each is back and down on beats seven and eight. Again, as they do so, they continue swinging their outside arm.

● They then get ready to repeat the move. It is normally repeated at least twice.

tuck turn to separate

The tuck turn is a basic move that is very similar to the tuck double turn on page 82.

This time, however, the woman turns only once.

● Start from a close-hold position as seen in previous moves.

● The man rocks the woman back on his left, her right.

● The man then replaces the weight back onto his right foot. The woman replaces the weight back onto her left foot as he begins to bring her in front.

● The man, kicking his left foot, tucks his left arm back in preparation for a turn.

■ beat one ▶ beat two ▶ beat three ▶

● The woman kicks down with her right foot as the man brings her around in front of him, pushing her right arm into his left.

beat four ▶

● The man kicks his right foot and lifts his left arm over the woman's head. As he does so, the woman follows his lead and turns over her right shoulder, kicking forward with her left foot.

beat five ▶

● The man brings his left arm and right foot down together. As he lowers his arm, the woman swings her left foot and body weight down.

beat six ▶

● Letting go of his partner, the man jumps into a "frog," or squat, position. As he releases her arm, the woman jumps into a "frog," or squat, position.

beat seven, beat eight ■

boogie back

This move is one of the breakaway steps and is usually performed in eight-count sequences, moving backward, after the partners have separated. It normally begins with the kick and clap of beat eight of the previous move.

● The man starts in a "frog," or squat, position. The woman starts in the same position.

● He kicks his right foot and claps at the same time on beat eight. She kicks with her right foot, also clapping on beat eight. They both do a ball change (see heel & toe, page 76–77), shuffling backward.

● On the half beat, the man steps back on the ball of his right foot. On beat one, he quickly steps back onto his left foot.

▶ **beat eight** ▶ **beat one** ▶

● On the half beat, the woman steps back on the ball of her right foot, and on beat one, she quickly steps back onto her left foot.

● Now the man kicks with his right foot on beat two. On the half beat, he steps back on the ball of his right foot. On beat three, he steps back onto his left foot.

● She now kicks her right foot on two. On the half beat, the woman steps back on the ball of her right foot, and on beat three, she steps back onto her left foot.

● The kick ball change is repeated four times in all to fit in time to a phrase of music.

beat one ▶ **beat two** ▶ **beat three** ▶ ■

boogie forward

This is another classic breakaway step. The movement often follows boogie backs and is a way for the couple to come back together again.

● The man brings his right foot in and imagines that he is about to draw a semicircle on the floor with his big toe.

● The woman brings her right foot in and imagines that she is about to draw a semicircle on the floor with her big toe

● The man then steps out on his right foot and pushes his hip diagonally forward over his right foot.

beat eight ▶ **beat eight** ▶ **beat one** ▶

● The woman then steps out on her right foot and pushes her hip diagonally forward over her right foot.

● The man now steps out on his left foot and pushes his hip diagonally forward over his left foot.

● The woman now steps out on her left foot and pushes her hip diagonally forward over her left foot.

● These movements are then repeated to make up eight beats of music. When they have finished one set of boogie forward, they may repeat another set of boogie backs.

beat one ▶ **beat two, beat three** ▶ **beat two, beat three** ▶ **repeat for four, five, six, seven** ■

lindy hop

shorty george

For this move, keep the weight forward on the toes, and let the heels come slightly off the floor. Keep the knees and feet more or less together all the time, and as you travel forward, make sure the toes of both feet are pointing forward at all times.

● The man kicks his right foot out to the side on eight, and brings knees and feet together (on the half beat). The woman also kicks her right foot out to the side on eight, and brings her knees and feet together (on the half beat).

beat eight

● The man takes a small step forward on his left foot, keeping his knees together while pushing them over to the left. At this point, his left arm is low and his right arm is high.

beat one

● The woman takes a small step forward on her left foot, keeping her knees together while pushing them over to the left. At this point, her left arm is low and her right arm is high.

beat one

- The man takes a very small step forward on the right, keeping his knees together while pushing them over to the right. Now his right arm is low and his left arm is high.

- The woman takes a very small step forward on the right, keeping her knees together while pushing them over to the right. Now her right arm is low and her left arm is high.

- These steps are now repeated by each partner on beats three through to seven. On beat seven, they can repeat the boogie backs.

- Alternatively, the man can continue stepping to beat eight while taking hold of his partner. The woman then freezes on beat seven and waits for the man to lead out on beat one of their next move.

beat two ▶ **beat two** **beats three to seven** ▶ **beat eight** ■

swing out

The swing out is a lindy turn in which you swing your partner out from a close-hold position. Those of you who have been around a little longer probably know lindy turns and lindy circles as swing outs as well.

● From a close-hold position, start with a Back Step as seen in previous moves. The woman's left hand rests on the man's right shoulder, her right hand in his left. His right hand rests under her right shoulder blade.

● The man turns his upper body toward the woman and takes his Back Step, which is the signal for her to take her Back Step. She offers some resistance with her right hand against his left.

● He now steps forward on his left foot in front of his partner and finishes facing her. The woman then replaces her weight onto her right foot.

● The man steps behind on his right foot, with his right arm under the woman's left shoulder blade.

beat one, beat two ▶ beat three, beat four ▶ beat three, beat four ▶

● When the man steps behind on his right foot, with his right arm under the woman's left shoulder blade, he pulls her forward.

● When the woman feels his hand pulling on her, she takes the first of two steps forward—on her left foot—in the direction of his pull.

● As the woman continues to step forward—now on her right foot—the man moves his right arm out of the way and steps around onto his left foot to face her.

● The man closes right to left to finish the turn and face his partner. The woman also turns to face the man, closing left to right.

beat five ▶ **beat five** ▶ **beat six** ▶ **beat seven, beat eight** ■

around the world

With this step, a good tip for the man to remember is to bring his right arm forward to meet the woman's shoulder as quickly as possible. Don't just lift your arm up and wait for her to run into it.

● As with changing places, the man and woman should have swapped positions by the end.

● Start with a Back Step in an open-hold position, with the woman's right hand in the man's left.

● As the man Back Steps onto his left foot, he replaces his weight onto his right foot and begins to lead the woman forward.

● As the man pulls the woman in close, she goes forward on her right foot, stepping past the man to his right.

beat one, beat two

beat three, beat four

● The man shifts his weight forward onto his left foot and places his right hand on the woman's left shoulder. The man keeps pulling the woman past his right side.

● As the man steps behind onto his right foot, he turns almost 180 degrees. The man sweeps his left hand over her head, letting go of her right hand at the highest point.

● The man continues turning over his right shoulder to step around onto his left foot on six. She takes three steps on beats five, six, and seven, left, right, left, to pivot around, completing a turn to her right over her right shoulder.

● He finishes the turn to face his partner on seven, eight. They are ready to continue.

beat three, beat four ▶ **beat five** ▶ **beat six, beat seven** ▶ **beat seven, beat eight** ■

heel & toe

This move finishes on a ball change, which is a quick shift of weight, stepping onto the ball of one foot on the half beat, and quickly changing weight onto the other foot on beat eight.

● Instead of the usual Back Step, the man points his left leg and right index finger toward his partner.

● The woman points her right leg and left index finger toward her partner. As they do so, each of them sits quite low on their supporting leg.

● The man then swings his left leg and his right arm backward, turning his head to the right.

● The woman swings her right leg and left arm backward, turning her head to the left.

● The man points his left leg and right index finger back toward the woman, repeating the move of beats one and two.

beat five, beat six

● The woman points her right leg and left index finger back toward the man, repeating the move of beats one and two.

beat five, beat six

● On beat seven, the man and the woman freeze position for a beat and a half.

beat seven

● They ball change to finish, with the man closing left to right, the woman closing right to left.

beat eight

heels

Heels is a styling variation that can be done by the man or the woman, independently or together, in place of the normal Back Step.

● Complete a regular Lindy turn and get ready to start a second Lindy turn. The man brings both feet together and bends at the knees, while swinging his free (right) arm up, then down, and rocking on his heels.

■ **beat one, beat two**

● The woman brings both feet together and bends at the knees, while swinging her free (left) arm up, then down, and rocking on her heels. Each drops the weight back onto their toes and continues the turn as normal.

beat one, beat two ▶

● Stepping forward onto his left foot, the man pulls the woman in toward him and begins to turn clockwise. At the same time, he places his right hand under her left shoulder blade.

beat three, beat four ▶

● As the man continues to pull the woman forward, she steps forward onto her right foot, turning her body parallel to his and placing her left hand on his right shoulder.

beat three, beat four ▶

● The man steps behind on his right foot and, with his right arm under the woman's left shoulder blade, he pulls her forward.

beat five ▶

● When the woman feels his hand pulling on her back, she takes the first of two steps forward—on her left foot—in the direction of his pull.

beat five ▶

● As the woman continues to step forward—now on her right foot—the man moves his right arm out of the way and steps around onto his left foot to face her.

beat six ▶

● The man closes right to left to finish the turn and face his partner. The woman also turns to face the man, closing left to right.

beat seven, beat eight ▶

kick away

Kick away is a styling variation that can be done by the man or the woman, independently or together, in place of the final beat seven, beat eight, and Back Step on beat one, beat two of the next lindy turn.

● Start with a Back Step. The man steps back onto his left foot and extends his left arm forward, bringing it back toward him as he replaces his weight onto his right foot. The woman steps back onto her right foot.

beat one, beat two

● As he begins to pull her forward, she replaces the weight onto her left foot. Stepping forward onto his left foot, the man pulls the woman in toward him and begins to turn clockwise.

beat three, beat four

● He places his right hand under her left shoulder blade. As he continues to pull her forward, she steps forward onto her right foot, turning parallel to him and placing her left hand on his right shoulder.

beat three, beat four

● The steps for beats five and six are exactly the same as for beats five and six of the lindy turn. See page 56

beat five, beat six

● Now leaning a little bit more toward each other, the man picks up his right knee and kicks forward. As he brings his foot back and down on eight, he turns away from his partner.

beat seven, beat eight ▶

● The woman picks up her left knee and kicks forward. As she brings her foot back and down on eight, she turns away from her partner.

beat seven, beat eight ▶

● Now leaning away from each other, the man picks up his left knee and kicks away. He pivots on his right foot, bringing his left foot back—but still up—to prepare traveling forward on three and four of the next lindy turn.

beat one, beat two ▶

● At the same time, the woman picks up her left knee and kicks away. She pivots on her right foot, bringing her left foot back—but still up—in preparation for traveling forward on three and four of the next lindy turn.

beat one, beat two ■

tuck double turn

When the woman takes her three steps on the double turn, she should keep her feet very close together. When the man is preparing to turn the woman under, he should think of bringing his left arm back toward his left ear before pushing.

● Start in a close hold with the woman's right hand in the man's left. His right arm is around her back, his hand resting just below her right shoulder blade.

● The man and woman then each take a Back Step as seen in previous moves.

● The man guides the woman in front of him, pushing with his right hand on her back. Pulling with his left hand. he shifts his weight onto his left foot. The woman then steps forward onto her right foot.

beat one ▸ **beat two** ▸ **beat three, beat four** ▸

● The man raises his left arm, while bringing his right foot to his left as he starts to turn the woman under the axis of his left hand.

beat five

● The woman then completes a double turn with three steps on beats five, six, and seven. The man keeps his arm above the lady's axis. He steps onto his left foot on beat six.

beat six

● The man steps on his right foot on beat seven. With the double turn complete, they face each other, the woman's right hand still clasped in his upraised left hand.

beat seven

● The man lowers his left arm, and the woman lowers her right in preparation for the next step.

beat eight

texas tommy

This move is sometimes known as the arm-breaker. The man must be very careful when taking the arm behind the woman's back to keep it very close to her back, pulling downward only. She should allow her arm to be taken fully behind her back to make the turn smoother.

● Start with the man and the woman taking a Back Step in an open hold as seen in previous moves.

● The man steps forward onto his left foot. He lifts his right arm up and forward, and pulls the woman into his right arm. Her left arm may rest lightly on his shoulder.

● As the man pulls the woman in, with a slightly bigger step than normal, she allows him to take her right arm behind her back. He changes the woman's hand from his left to his right behind her back.

beat one, beat two ▸ **beat three, beat four** ▸ **beat three, beat four** ▸

● As the man steps behind on his right foot, the woman starts to unwind on beat five.

● The man steps around toward the woman on his left foot, pulling slightly down. She continues to turn around to the right on beat six.

● The man steps around onto his right foot, and lets the woman continue unwinding on the spot.

● She finishes the turn on beat seven on her left foot. Through beats five, six, and seven, she keeps her feet close together.

beat five ▶ **beat six** ▶ **beat seven, beat eight** ▶ **beat seven, beat eight** ■

intermediate

hand-to-hand charleston

lindy hop

This is a classic sequence of steps in which the man repeats the hand-to-hand charleston twice before going into a kick around followed by a back charleston. Both the man and the woman swap hands as they change direction.

● When you kick, do not flex or point the foot, but leave it relaxed somewhere in the middle.

● Start in a shaking-hands position as seen in previous moves, with the woman's right hand in the man's right hand.

● The man turns slightly to his left, picks up his right knee, and kicks toward the left corner. The woman turns slightly to her left, picks up her right knee, and kicks toward the left corner.

● As the man brings his foot back, he keeps his knee in the air and pivots on his left foot to face the right corner. The woman brings her foot back, keeping the knee in the air, and pivots to face the right corner.

■ ▶ **beat one, beat two** ▶ **beat two** ▶

● The man now kicks his right foot toward the right corner. The woman kicks her right foot toward the right corner.

● The man now puts his right foot down. The woman also puts her right foot down. He picks up his left knee and kicks toward the right corner. She picks up her left knee and kicks toward the right corner.

● As the man brings his left foot back, he pivots on his right foot to face the left corner, still with his left knee in the air. The woman brings her left foot back and pivots on her right foot to face the right corner, left knee in air.

● The man kicks his left foot to the left corner. The woman kicks her left foot to the left corner. He brings his foot down, and she brings her foot down. They are now ready to repeat.

beat three, beat four ▶ **beat five, beat six** ▶ ▶ **beat seven, beat eight** ■

transition to a kick around

Having now completed the hand-to-hand charleston (see previous page), you are now ready to do another hand-to-hand charleston that will segue effortlessly into a kick around.

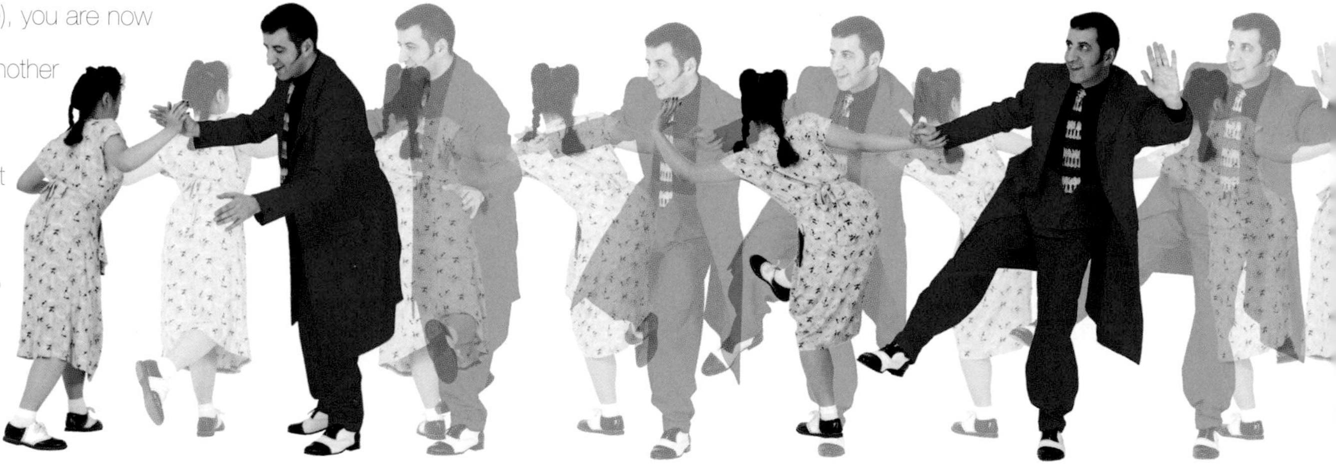

● The man again turns slightly to his left, picks up his right knee, and kicks toward the left corner. The woman turns slightly to her left, picks up her right knee, and kicks toward the left corner.

● As the man brings his foot back, he keeps his knee in the air, and pivots on his left foot to face the right corner.

● The woman brings her foot back, keeping the knee in the air, and pivots to face the right corner.

beat one

beat two

● The man now kicks his right foot toward the right corner. The woman kicks her right foot toward the right corner and then down

● He then picks up his left knee, and kicks toward the right corner.

● She picks up her left knee, and kicks toward the right corner.

● They are now ready to continue with the kick around as shown on the next page.

beat three, beat four ▶ **beat five** ▶ ▶ **beat six** ■

the kick around

This move is an exit step from the previous hand-to-hand charleston. It begins on what are, in effect, the last two steps of a normal hand-to-hand charleston.

● As the man brings his left foot back, he pivots on his right foot counterclockwise over his left shoulder, preparing to use four kicks to get around.

● As he starts the kick around, he pushes off his partner. This gives the woman the signal to start her kick around.

● The man starts turning counter-clockwise over his left shoulder, kicking his left foot. The woman turns counterclockwise over her left shoulder.

beat seven, beat eight

● To give the correct look: if the woman kicks with her right leg, she throws her right arm in the air. If she kicks with her left, she throws her left arm in the air.

● If the man kicks with his right leg, he throws his right arm in the air. If he kicks with his left, he throws his left arm in the air.

● The man continues turning counterclockwise, putting his left foot down, and then kicking his right foot out and down.

● The woman continues turning counterclockwise, putting her left foot down, and then kicking her right foot out and down.

▶ ▶ **beat eight, beat one** ▶ **beat two** ▶

the kick around into back charleston

In this move, the woman mustn't forget to look for her partner as she kicks around. When the man offers his hand, that is the signal to exit.

● This move continues directly on from beat two of the kick around on the previous page.

● The man continues kicking around on his left foot. The woman continues kicking around on her left foot.

● The man offers his right hand for the woman to take with her right hand as he finishes his last kick on the right foot.

● As the woman finishes her kick around, she should spot the man's right hand, and place her right hand on top of his.

▸ **beat three, beat four** **beat five, beat six** ▸ ▸

● The woman continues the kick around until they end up facing the same direction in a tandem-like position. Looking straight ahead, she points her left foot back.

● Now, with both partners facing the same direction, the man points his left foot back and pushes his left arm forward. This is the first step of a back charleston.

● Both partners should maintain the "C" shape throughout the whole movement.

● The woman should have her hands on top, with her palms down. The man should have his hands underneath, his palms up.

beat seven, beat eight ▶ ▶ ▶

back charleston

When kicking behind or in front, try to kick slightly toward the corners—left foot to left corner, right foot to right corner. That way, there shouldn't be any painful mistakes if you're going in different directions.

● Continuing directly on from the previous move, both partners are now in a tandem position.

● With a small lean forward of the upper body, the man has pointed his left foot back, left arm forward, and right arm back. The woman has done exactly the same, her left hand in his left hand.

beat seven, beat eight

● The man now kicks his left foot forward and down. The woman kicks her left foot forward and down. They both then reverse arms—right arm forward, left arm back.

beat one, beat two

● Now preparing for a double kick, first the man kicks his right foot forward without putting his foot down. The woman kicks her right foot forward without putting her feet down.

beat three, beat four

● The man reverses arms again—right arm back, left arm forward. The woman reverses arms again—right arm back, left arm forward.

● The man then kicks behind. At the same time, the woman also kicks behind.

● The man reverses arms again—right arm forward, left arm back. The woman reverses arms again—right arm forward, left arm back.

● The man puts his right foot down. The woman puts her right foot down. They are now ready to repeat the sequence.

beat five, beat six

beat six

charleston lift

This move should really only be attempted if both partners are used to practicing with each other because the woman jumps while the man lifts. It can be dangerous if your timing is not 100 percent synchronized.

● Start with the man behind the woman, each of them bending forward at the waist, and left foot slightly raised. He holds both of her hands, pushing them slightly forward at waist level.

● Both Back Step, left, right. As they do so, the man raises the woman's arms up and out by her sides as a pre-signal for the lift.

● They go down, bringing their feet together as the man lowers the woman's arms, bringing her hands in close to her hips. He keeps his hands under hers, ready to lift her.

beat seven, beat eight

beat one, beat two

● As the man straightens up, with both feet close together, the woman leaps into the air, pulling both legs up under her as he pushes her up by the hands. The woman should bring her knees up toward her chest.

● As the woman comes back down to earth again on both feet, the man returns to his forward squat position while still keeping a firm hold of her hands.

● The man points his left foot back, and he is now ready to continue.

● The woman points her left foot back. As they lean farther forward, the man pushes her left arm just forward of her body, and pulls her right arm back.

beat three, beat four ▸ ▸

beat five, beat six ▸

beat seven, beat eight ▸

charleston exit into jig walk

In this move, when the man wants his partner to turn out, he must clearly let go of his left hand with a forward motion. At the same time, he pushes the woman around with his right hand in a U-shaped motion, swapping hands at the last moment.

● This continues directly on from the end of the charleston lift or a regular charleston. They both finish the charleston with their left foot back.

● As the man kicks his left forward, he lets go of the woman's left arm. She turns sideways in front of him, kicking forward with her left foot.

● The man passes the woman's hand from his right to his left while kicking forward with his right foot.

●The man then Back Steps onto his left foot; then replaces his weight onto his right foot. The woman Back Steps onto her right foot. She then replaces her weight onto her left foot.

●The man pulls the woman toward him, and he kicks outside with his left foot, while she kicks inside his feet with her right foot.

●As they continue to move toward each other, the man kicks inside with his right foot and the woman kicks outside with her left.

●They finish in a close-hold position with his right arm around her back and her left arm on his shoulder.

beat five, beat six ▶ **beat seven, beat eight** ▶ **beat one, beat two** ▶ ■

jig walk lift

This is a fun and easy air step. If the woman jumps and the man lifts at exactly the same time, it can look very spectacular. It's all a matter of timing—and practice, of course.

● This move can continue on directly from the end of the charleston exit into jig walk above or from a Back Step.

● In a close-hold position, the man kicks outside with his left foot while the woman kicks inside with her right.

● The man kicks inside with his right foot while the woman kicks inside with her left foot.

● The man repeats a Back Step on his left, then right foot, pushing the woman back on her right, then left foot.

● The man steps down close to his partner, and she steps forward in preparation for the lift.

● The woman jumps up (knees outside her partner), pushing down with her right hand in the man's left and her left arm on his right shoulder. He lifts her, supporting her with both arms.

● The lift is straight up and down, with the man using his legs to lift and support his partner, not his back. She must remember to take a small bounce in the knees when she lands.

beat five, beat six ▶ **beat seven, beat eight** **beat one, beat two** **beat three, beat four** ■

hollywood swing

send out

Hollywood swing is a style in which partners must aim to counterbalance each other. This, in turn, creates a tension—a rubber-band effect— between the man and woman. As with the lindy hop, triple steps often replace the single slow steps.

● Start in a V-shaped close-hold position, with the man's weight sitting over his right leg. The woman's weight is sitting over her left leg.

● The man rocks forward onto his left foot for beats one and two; then back onto his right foot three and four. The woman rocks forward onto her right foot for one and two, and back onto her left for three and four.

● The man steps forward onto his left foot on beat five; and replaces the weight onto his right foot on six, but still leaning forward. At the same time, he leads the woman into a regular Back Step.

beat one, beat two

beat three, beat four

beat five

● The woman takes a Back Step onto her right foot on beat five, then replaces her weight onto her left foot on six. She needs to push her back into the man's hand to create the momentum for the send out.

● The man shifts his weight over his left foot and leans in that direction. With his right hand firmly on the woman's back, he pushes her forward. He also thinks about pointing his left arm in the direction she is going.

● The woman runs forward onto her right foot and into her own right arm. She doesn't turn back to face the man until the last possible moment.

● The man shifts his weight back onto his right foot. The woman pivots around onto her left foot to face her partner once again.

beat six **beat seven, beat eight** ▶ **beat one, beat two** ■

walk through

This move is very similar to changing places, though the styling completely changes the look. When stepping, both the man and the woman want to sit a little deeper over each foot. This is known as anchoring the weight. The partners use their arms to create the rubber-band effect, and the woman delays turning until the last possible moment.

● Start in an open-hold position, with the woman's right hand in the man's left.

● The man does a Back Step onto his left foot, but pulls the woman toward him. The woman steps forward onto her right foot.

● As the man replaces his weight onto his right foot, the woman continues stepping forward on her left. He uses his raised left hand to pull the woman past his right hip.

● The man raises his left hand higher so the woman's head can pass under it as she moves past. As she does so, he steps forward, shifting his weight onto his left foot.

● With her right hand still held in his left, he lowers her arm as she runs into it, which makes her turn back to face the man.

● The woman then pivots on her left foot to face the man again. The man steps onto his right leg as he leans away from his partner.

● They face each other once more, with the woman's right hand in the man's left.

sugar push

This is a very common step in the Hollywood swing repertoire. The woman can add some flourish to this move by adding a swivel in the direction of the foot she is stepping on when she takes two straight walking steps forward.

● Start in an open-hold position, with the woman's right hand in the man's left.

● When the man takes his Back Step, the woman takes two small forward steps.

● She can add a little swivel, right, left, in the direction she is stepping when she has had more practice.

● The man then offers his right hand, which the woman takes in her left hand.

● With both hands now in his, the woman steps forward onto her right foot as he steps forward on his left.

● As the woman moves closer to the man, he creates a block, and pulling both arms out to the side, he creates a small pyramid shape between them. She leans in close to the man's chest.

● The woman then shifts her weight back onto her left foot. He shifts backward onto his right foot, as he brings his arms together and pushes her away.

● At the finish of the move, they can return to their starting positions, but now with a double-hand hold.

beat five, beat six

whip leader

This is a very dynamic move, and the more each partner can sit into each foot to create the rubber-band effect, the better it will look. Beats three and four, and seven and eight are frequently dancedwith the triple timing described on page 13.

● Start with your weight sitting back on your right foot. Take a Back Step onto your left foot.

● At the same time, pull your partner forward, replacing the weight onto your right foot.

● As your partner is coming forward, step forward onto your left foot. As she passes you on your right-hand side, follow her around.

● Finish up in an almost 180-degree turn, with your weight anchored over your left foot.

● Step behind 180 degrees on your right foot. Your foot, hip, and shoulder must all turn at the same time. Your weight is now anchored over your right foot, and your right shoulder is leaning to the right.

● Shift your weight back onto your left foot while turning to face your partner.

● Finish, closing left to right on seven, eight, back in your starting position once more.

▶ **beat five**

▶ **beat six**

▶ **beat seven, beat eight** ■

whip follower

The woman's steps on beats one, two, and seven can either be done straight, or she can add a little decoration with a swivel as seen here.It's up to the woman to decide how big or small to make the swivel. Beats three and four, and seven and eight are frequently danced with the triple timing described on page 13.

● Facing your partner, start with your weight sitting back on your left foot.

● When the man pulls you forward, take two small steps forward, swiveling right, left.

● Step forward on your right foot, pivoting around on your right almost 180 degrees to face your partner.

● Now step out onto your left foot, directly opposite your partner.

● At the same time, anchor your weight over your left foot to match your partner.

● Continue turning in the same direction, stepping backward on your right foot facing your partner.

● Finish, closing left to right on seven, eight, back in your starting position once more.

beat five ▶ **beat six** ▶ **beat seven, beat eight** ■

whip partners

To create the right feel for the Hollywood styling, the partners should stand facing each other, her right hand in his left. Keeping the arms a mirror image, they imagine they are going to sit down together and then pull away to create the rubber-band tension.

● The man starts with his weight sitting back on his right foot. He takes a Back Step onto his left foot. The woman starts with her weight sitting back on her left foot.

● The man pulls the woman forward, replacing the weight onto his right foot. As he does so, she takes two small steps forward, swiveling right, left.

● As the woman comes forward, the man steps forward onto his left foot. As she passes him on his right-hand side, he follows her around.

beat one, beat two ▶ ▶ **beat three, beat four** ▶

● The woman steps forward on her right foot, pivoting around on her right almost 180 degrees to face her partner. He finishes up in an almost 180-degree turn, with his weight anchored over his left foot.

▶ **beat five**

● The man steps behind 180 degrees onto his right foot—hip, shoulder, and foot turning simultaneously. His weight is anchored over his right foot, and his right shoulder leans to the right.

▶ **beat six**

● The woman steps out onto her left foot, directly opposite the man. He shifts his weight back onto his left foot, turning to face her. She continues turning, stepping backward onto her right foot, facing him.

▶ **beat seven, beat eight**

● They finish, closing left to right on seven, eight, back in their starting positions once more. ■

whip with shoulder release

This move is esentially the same as the whip from beat one through to five. On beat six, there is a free spin styling variation for the woman.

● The man starts this move with his weight sitting back on his right foot. The woman starts with her weight sitting back on her left foot.

● The man takes a Back Step onto his left foot. He pulls the woman forward, replacing the weight onto his right foot

● As he does so, she takes two small steps forward, swiveling right, left.

● As the woman comes forward, the man steps forward onto his left foot. As she passes him on his right-hand side, he follows her around.

● The woman steps forward on her right foot, pivoting around on her right almost 180 degrees to face her partner. He finishes up in an almost 180-degree turn, with his weight anchored over his left foot.

● The man steps behind 180 degrees onto his right foot—hip, shoulder, and foot turning simultaneously. His weight is anchored over his right foot, and his right shoulder leans to the right.

● The man keeps his right hand on the woman's back and releases his left hand. As she steps back on six, he allows her to roll off his right hand. She makes one complete turn to come back to face her partner.

● They finish, closing left to right on seven, eight, back in their starting positions once more.

beat five

beat six

beat seven, beat eight

swivels

This move can be repeated as many times as you like until you are ready to exit. Here it is repeated for another four beats after beats seven, eight.

● The man starts with his weight over his right foot, sitting lower than usual into his right leg. He points his left toe out to the side on beat one and closes left to right, replacing his weight onto his left foot on beat two.

● On beat one, the man's left hand should be pointing directly at the center of his partner. He makes a small semicircular movement to the left. On two, he brings the hand back to the center in a reverse movement.

● The woman starts with her weight on her left foot. As the man leads, she can either do a straight swivel or a kick ball change on her right foot, emphasizing the kick with a twist. on beat two.

● For the kick ball change, she kicks the right foot on beat one, twisting to the right. She brings her feet back together and the ball of her right foot down, swiveling to the left on two.

● The man points his right foot out to the side on beat three and closes right to left, replacing his weight again onto his right foot on beat four—repeating the exact same arm lead to the left as just described.

● During the swivels, the man turns slowly to his right, staying on the spot. He leads the woman around him in a circular motion to his right, her left.

● As the woman swivels around the man, she needs to keep her torso directly behind her hand. She must not allow her arm to end up out to the side of her body.

● The man repeats steps one to four for five, six, seven, and eight. The woman repeats steps one, two for steps three, four, five, six, seven, and eight.

beat three, beat four ▶ ▶ ▶ ■

advanced

hollywood kicks

hollywood swing

This move consists of a Back Step followed by six kicks on alternating feet. It's a good idea to try this without any turns first.

● Start in a V-shaped, close-hold position. The man takes a Back Step, left, right on one, two. The woman takes a Back Step right, left on one, two.

beat one, beat two

● The man kicks his left foot toward the woman, but on the outside of her right foot. She kicks toward him, between his legs.

beat three, beat four

● The man turns out and rolls away from the woman, kicking away on beat five with his right foot. She kicks away from him with her left foot. As they both put their foot down on six, he rotates her 180 degrees.

beat five, beat six

● The woman sits almost horizontally on the man's right hip, low down on her left foot, holding onto him with her left arm. He then kicks his left foot on seven, eight. She kicks with her left foot on seven, eight.

beat seven, beat eight

● He then kicks with his right foot on one, two. She kicks with her left foot on one, two.

● The man kicks again with his left foot on three four, and lifts his partner up, turning her to face him.

● She kicks in between his legs with her right foot, as he brings her up to standing position.

● The man kicks between her legs with his right foot. The woman kicks outside his right leg with her left foot.

beat one, beat two ▶ **beat three, beat four** ▶ **beat five, beat six** ■

advanced

cradle with pecks

With this move, the man should always make sure he has plenty of space around him before he starts swinging his partner about.

● Start in a V-shaped, close-hold position. As the man and woman Back Step on one, two, he goes very low into his right leg, preparing to lift her, and gives extra support with his arms. She prepares to jump onto his lap.

● The man swings the woman up in front of his chest and then down onto his lap. She must jump onto him and not just into his arms.

● The man must make a very firm base with his feet—slightly wider than shoulder width—and pull the woman close to him with his right arm. With her left arm on his right shoulder, she pulls herself close and lands on his lap.

beat one, beat two ▶ **beat three, beat four** ▶ **beat five, beat six** ▶

● They now add a very old, classic step called peckin'. The man goes right, then left, right. Puckering his lips, he pecks like a chicken on each side of his head.

beat seven, beat eight ▶

● The woman does the same. They repeat these steps for beats one, two, three, four.

beats one, two, three, four

● Using his legs for power, the man lifts her off. As he lifts her, she keeps the tension in her arms, her shoulders down, and imagines she is lifting her stomach throughout the whole movement.

beat five, beat six ▶

● The man brings the woman back down to his side, supporting her with both arms. When she lands, she takes a little bounce in the knees.

beat seven, beat eight ■

quick stop

I was taught this step by Jean Veloz, who danced it in several movies, including *Groovy Movie* (1944), a Pete Smith specialty. Jean called the move the "deep freeze."

● The man starts with his weight sitting back on his right foot. He takes a Back Step onto his left foot. The woman starts with her weight sitting back on her left foot.

● The man pulls the woman forward, replacing the weight onto his right foot. As he does so, she takes two small steps forward, swiveling right, left.

● As the woman comes forward, the man steps forward onto his left foot. As she passes him on his right-hand side, he follows her around. He finishes up in an almost 180-degree turn, with his weight anchored over his left foot.

● The woman steps forward on her right foot, pivoting around on her right almost 180 degrees to face her partner.

beat one, beat two ▶

beat three, beat four ▶

● The man extends his left arm to his left side slightly. The woman turns 90 degrees, stepping onto her left foot.

● The man shifts his weight onto his left foot on six. At the same time, he sweeps his left arm over her head. She steps onto her right foot with her right arm above her head.

● With her weight mainly over the right foot (leaving her left foot where it is), she pivots on the ball of her right foot another 180 degrees back to face her partner.

● She pushes her hips away from him, taking a deep bend in the right knee. As she completes the turn, he quickly lowers his left arm, sitting his weight back away from his partner, counter-balancing her lean away from him.

beat five, beat six ▶ **beat seven, beat eight** ▶ ■

index